WORLD RELIGIONS

BUDDHISM

Catherine Hewitt

RSVP
**RAINTREE
STECK-VAUGHN**
PUBLISHERS
The Steck-Vaughn Company

Austin, Texas

Words appearing in *italic* have not fallen into common English usage. The publishers have followed Merriam Webster's Collegiate Dictionary (Tenth Edition) for spelling and usage.

Library of Congress Cataloging-in-Publication Data
Hewitt, Catherine.
Buddhism / Catherine Hewitt.
        p.   cm.—(World religions)
Includes bibliographical references and index.
Summary: An illustrated history and explanation of the beliefs and practices of Buddhism.
ISBN 0-8172-5291-6
1. Buddhism—Juvenile literature. [1. Buddhism.]
I. Title. II. Series: World religions (Thomson Learning)
BQ4032.H49   1995
294.3—dc20   95-1942

Printed in Italy. Bound in the United States.
2 3 4 5 6 7 8 9 0 02 01 00 99 98

Cover photo: A monk in Bangkok
Title page: Prayer flags, Ladakh
Contents page: Borobudur, Malaysia

Acknowledgments

The author is most grateful for the help given by the following as she wrote this book: Sister Sundara of Amaravati, Martine Batchelor, Jeanne Bendik, Shirley MacDonald, Ron Maddox, Medhina, Sati Sati, Burt Taylor, Geshe Tashi, Jisu Sunim.

The author and publishers thank the following for their permission to reproduce photographs: Sally Ash: p. 17; Chithurst Buddhist Monastery: 23, 35; Eye Ubiquitous: *cover* (D. Brannigan), 29 (t), 30 (JCW), 32 (D. Cumming), 45; Robert Harding Picture Library: pp. 31, 33, 42 (Elly Beintema); Christine Osborne: pp. 5 (b), 10, 11 (t), 24, 44; Joan Peatty: p. 27; Spink & Son: p. 22; TRIP: *title page* (F. Good), *contents page* (W. Jacobs), 4 (t) (J. Wakelin), 5 (t) (I. Corse), 6 (J. Wakelin), 7 (A. and B. Peerless), 8 (H. Rogers), 9 (A. and B. Peerless), 11 (b) (Dinodia Picture Agency), 12 (T. Noorits), 13 (t) (A. Di Nola), 13 (b) (W. Jacobs), 16 (W. Jacobs), 18 (t) (R. Cracknell), 18 (b) (T. Moorse), 21 (J. Batten), 28 (R. Powers), 29 (b) (J. Moscrop), 36 (H. Rogers), 39 (t) (A. Di Nola), 39 (b) (W. Jacobs), 41 (J. Moscrop), 43 (J. Wakelin); Beatrice Varma: p. 38; Paul Woods: p. 37.

Contents

THE FOUR NOBLE TRUTHS

At his first sermon the Buddha taught:

- There is suffering.

- The cause of suffering is wanting.

- Suffering can end completely.

- The Eightfold Path is the cure.

Sometimes the Buddha (which means "the enlightened one") is called a skilled doctor. He tells people what is wrong, what has caused the trouble, and that they can be cured if they follow his advice.

INTRODUCTION

Siddhartha, an Indian prince who lived more than two thousand five hundred years ago, found peace, or enlightenment, within himself. His teachings on how to achieve this peace became the foundation of Buddhism.

A young pilgrim contemplates a Buddha image in Shikoku, Japan.

Prince Siddhartha knew how alike we are. Everyone can feel happy and confident but also sad, lonely, and afraid. People have these feelings now, as they have through the ages. Prince Siddhartha called this suffering *dukkha*. This Indian word means any unpleasant feeling, from a little irritation to great sadness.

Siddhartha left his luxurious palace, his family, and his friends to search for the cause and the cure of the suffering. At last he was enlightened, and he spent the rest of his life teaching the Four Noble Truths. The cause of suffering is wanting (called *tanha*): wanting good things never to change, wanting bad things to go away, and wanting to have everything one wishes for. The cure, says the Buddha, is to follow the Eightfold Path, which is also called the Middle Way.

All eight aspects of the Middle Way come into everyday life:

Buddhists try to accept the teaching about *dukkha*.

They strive to think unselfishly and compassionately.

They try to tell the truth and speak in a way that is helpful.

Buddha statue, Nepal.

They try to be kind and thoughtful in all they do.

They choose work that is useful and will not damage people or the environment.

They make an effort to live wisely and encourage good.

They try to be mindful, which means being alert and aware of what they are thinking, feeling, and doing, so that they do not behave in a way that they will later regret.

They meditate. Meditation is an important part of the Buddha's teaching. When a Buddhist meditates, he remains quiet and still, feeling his breath going in and out. This helps him to allow his mind and body to be peaceful. He will see his thoughts and moods begin and end. What a person chooses to do begins with a thought in his or her mind. A person needs to choose well.

THE EIGHTFOLD PATH

When Buddhists choose the Eightfold Path, they try to develop the following:

Right Understanding

Right Thought

Right Speech

Right Action

Right Work

Right Effort

Right Mindfulness

Right Meditation

These Sri Lankan nuns wear the white robes of novices, for women cannot yet be ordained.

THE THREE REFUGES

- I take refuge in the Buddha

- I take refuge in the dharma (teaching)

- I take refuge in the *sangha*

Inside a Buddhist temple in busy Bangkok, a monk and a layman show respect to the Buddha.

People who followed the Buddha during his lifetime became monks and nuns, as do Buddhist followers today. The community of monks and nuns is called the *sangha*, and there is a strong and practical relationship between the *sangha* and lay Buddhists.

When the first followers became Buddhists, they asked for the Three Refuges, also called the Three Jewels or the Three Treasures.

Today, when Buddhists go to a monastery, they kneel before the shrine, put their hands together in a way called *anjali*, bow, and request the Three Refuges. A monk chants the words and the others repeat them. It is also possible to take the Refuges in one's own mind when one is alone.

The Buddha's teaching is called the dharma. All those who follow it strive to be contented and peaceful, not harming people or any other living beings. They wish to live with everyone in friendliness and understanding. The Middle Way helps them in everything they do; meditation and mindfulness help them watch their thoughts and feelings. They believe in the knowledge that wise thoughts lead to good actions.

1

THE STORY OF BUDDHISM

Prince Siddhartha

Siddhartha Gautama was born in Lumbini, possibly in 563 B.C.E. (see page 47). It is impossible to know exact dates of events from so long ago. His parents were rulers of a small kingdom in northeastern India.

A week after he was born, his mother, Queen Maya, died, and Siddhartha was brought up by his aunt, Pajapati. When a wise man predicted that the child would become either a great king or a renowned holy man, King Suddhodana was determined to make sure that his precious son grew up to be a king, not a homeless wanderer. Therefore Siddhartha lived a life of luxury and pleasure, guarded from ugliness and sadness and always surrounded by beautiful people and objects. He could have been spoiled and arrogant, but in fact he was gentle and thoughtful.

The northern Indian town of Lumbini, where Siddhartha was born, is today in Nepal. Bodh Gaya was the place of his enlightenment. He died in Kushinagara.

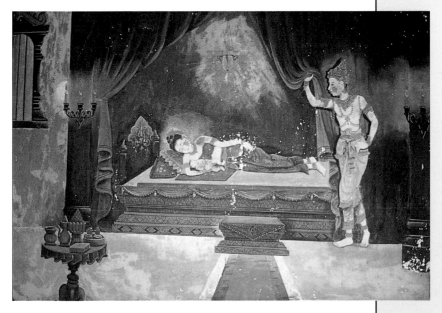

This fresco from Chiang Mai, Thailand, shows Prince Siddhartha leaving his wife, Yasodhara, and their baby son to go to search for an answer to his questions about life outside the palace.

7

Although he had everything that money could buy, Siddhartha was uneasy. When he was 29 years old, he decided to escape from his palace to see the world outside.

It was difficult to leave his wife and baby son with his father and aunt, but silently Siddhartha left the palace. He cut off his hair and changed his fine clothes for the robes of a wandering, homeless monk. This major change in Siddhartha's life is called the Great Renunciation.

This action changed his life. On separate occasions, he saw a sick man, an old man, a dead man, and a holy man. These are called the Four Heavenly Messengers. Siddhartha saw that his life in the palace had hidden him from hard reality: that old age, sickness, and death come to everyone. Remembering the serene calm of the holy man, he felt that *he* knew the truth about life. His must be the way to follow.

As he sat beneath the Bo tree, Siddhartha, within his own mind, was tempted by Mara, the Buddhist devil. Mara showed the prince how he could be a rich, famous, mighty king. Siddhartha resisted every temptation. As he saw the morning star, the Buddha touched the earth as witness to his enlightenment. This wall painting at a monastery is a modern interpretation of the temptations.

The search for enlightenment

Living and traveling in the forest, Siddhartha listened to famous religious teachers, but they could not give him the final truth he was seeking. He joined five ascetics, men who deliberately went without food and sleep. Almost dying of hunger, he decided that ill-treating the body was not the way for him to achieve wisdom. He accepted some rice and his five friends left him, thinking him weak and soft. It was now six years since his Renunciation.

After his strength returned, Siddhartha resolved to meditate until he knew the truth about the cause of suffering and the way to end it. He sat beneath a sacred tree at Bodh

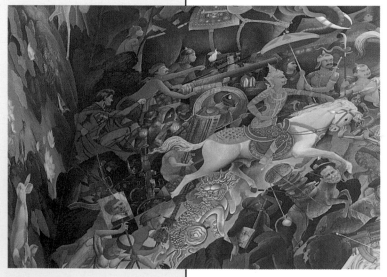

Gaya and at long last entered a state of perfect joy and peace, called nirvana. In this state of bliss he understood the Four Noble Truths about suffering; he was now the Buddha, which means the "awakened" or "enlightened" one, "the one who knows."

This buddharupa *(statue of the Buddha) is at the Shwedagon Pagoda in Rangoon, Myanmar. The Buddha touches the earth as a sign of his enlightenment.*

A wandering teacher

For 45 years—until his death—the Buddha traveled through India, teaching people what he had learned about the nature of human existence and how they could be freed from their suffering. His first followers were the five ascetics who had abandoned him earlier. His family, too, accepted his teaching and his aunt, Pajapati, became the first Buddhist nun. The community of monks and nuns who followed the Buddha was called the *sangha.*

Many people joined the Buddha as monks, called *bhikkshus*, and later also as nuns, called *bhikkshunis*. They lived austere lives, wearing simple robes, eating only one meal a day from the food that people gave them, and asking only for medicine and for shelter for the night. A set of rules was made to help the members of the *sangha* live without causing any harm to people or the environment. These rules, called the *Vinaya*, are followed to this day.

During the rainy season, called *vassa*, the *sangha* could not travel, and so they built shelters called *viharas* where they could stay, meditating and studying.

EMPEROR ASOKA

Asoka ruled over a huge empire in India, from approximately 265 to 238 B.C.E. He was a warrior king until he heard the dharma. Then he was horrified at the bloodshed he had caused and vowed to live by the Buddha's teaching. He became a compassionate ruler, caring for the poor, making just laws, and living peacefully with his neighbors. He provided homes, education, and medical treatment. Animals also were protected and received medicine. The king discouraged hunting.

There was religious freedom. King Asoka wanted people to live together in harmony. All over his huge empire, he had carved the words of the dharma on rocks and pillars for his subjects to see. Through his enthusiasm, Buddhism was spread to many lands, to which he sent teachers.

The death of the Buddha

At 80 years old, the Buddha knew he was dying. He would not be reborn, because he had been enlightened and would now enter nirvana forever. He told his sorrowing friends not to grieve. All things change. They must practice being mindful so as to become enlightened. He died peacefully at Kushinagara, and his death is called the *parinirvana*, the final entry into nirvana.

Huge reclining buddharupas, *like this one at Polonnaruwa, Sri Lanka, represent the Buddha entering nirvana.*

The spread of Buddhism in India

After the Buddha's death, the *sangha* continued traveling and teaching. As more people were ordained, many chose to live in cities as scholars, writers, and teachers, while others became forest *bhikkshus*. The *sangha* met periodically to decide on matters of teaching and discipline.

In about the first century C.E., great changes in the teaching developed as new sermons and ideas about the Buddha were introduced. The new form of Buddhism was named Mahayana, which means the "great vehicle." In contrast, the old form of Buddhism was called Hinayana, the "small vehicle." One sect within Hinayana was Theravada, and today Theravada is a major tradition of Buddhism.

Buddhism in Asia

At a Buddhist meeting at Pataliputra (modern-day Patna) during the reign of King Asoka, it was decided to send missionaries to Sri Lanka and other countries. The spread of Buddhism outside India began.

In 242 B.C.E. Asoka sent his son, Bhikkhu Mahinda, to teach the dharma in Sri Lanka. The King of Sri Lanka became a Buddhist, as did thousands of his followers, and many men became *bhikkshus*. Women also wished to join the *sangha*, and so King Asoka's daughter, Bhikkhuni Sanghamitta, sailed to the island in order to ordain *bhikkshunis*. She took a sapling from the Bo tree, which was planted at Anuradhapura, and the tree still flourishes there today.

By the eleventh century C.E., Buddhism had declined in influence in India, but it flourished in many other Asian countries. It was adapted to different ways of life in different countries and became merged with other religions, so new styles of Buddhism arose.

A sacred Bo tree at Anuradhapura

This Tibetan boy is a tulku, *the reincarnation of a renowned lama. He was discovered and passed many tests. Now he is being trained for his future responsibilities.*

Dalai Lamas and Tibetan Buddhists

Buddhist teachers from Nepal and China introduced the religion to Tibet in the seventh century, but it was about 775 that an Indian monk set up the first monastery there. A particular style of Tibetan Buddhism, called Vajrayana, developed, with monks known as lamas (teachers). In the fourteenth century a sect called the Gelugpas was established. Its chief abbot was the Dalai Lama (*Dalai* meaning "great as the ocean"). From the middle of the seventeenth century until 1950, each Dalai Lama was not only a spiritual leader but also ruler of Tibet. He lived in the Potala Palace in the holy city of Lhasa.

The Dalai Lama in Estonia. He travels widely to remind the world of his people's situation. In 1989 he was awarded the Nobel Peace Prize for his nonviolent attempts to free Tibet. He gave all the prize money to the Tibetan refugees.

The fourteenth Dalai Lama was only five years old when he was recognized as the reincarnation of the thirteenth Dalai Lama and enthroned in the Potala Palace in 1940. He then received long and rigorous training as a monk. However, his rulership of Tibet came to an end when the country was invaded by Communist China in 1950. Nine years later, to escape Chinese repression, the Dalai Lama and a hundred thousand refugees fled to Dharamsala in north India, and today Tibetan refugees are living in exile in many other countries as well. From their base in Dharamsala, the Tibetans try to preserve their cultural and spiritual heritage.

Buddhism in the Western world

In the nineteenth century, Buddhism began to have an influence in Western countries. Western scholars whose countries had colonies in the Indian subcontinent and Southeast Asia began to study and write about the religion. In the twentieth century Westerners visited Buddhist countries to learn more, and Buddhists traveled to the West to work and teach. Today most Western countries have scattered Buddhist groups and some large temples. Centers have been formed for those who wish to practice a more Western style of Buddhism.

Today, there are many forms of Buddhism around the world. However, in spite of all the differences, the original teaching of the Buddha remains central to every tradition.

2

THE WORLD OF BUDDHISM

Buddhism is a major religion in Asia. In some countries, including Sri Lanka and Thailand, Buddhists follow the older, Theravada form of the religion. In others, Mahayana has developed different, distinctive styles, including Zen Buddhism.

There are also many small centers of Buddhism, of all traditions, all over the world. In particular, the practice of meditation is spreading in the West.

The Burmese are Theravada Buddhists. They visit the Shwedagon Pagoda in Rangoon.

The Red Hat sect is one of several orders of Tibetan Buddhism. For ceremonies, senior members of all except the Gelugpa order wear red hats.

CANADA

UNITED STATES

EUROPE

SOUTH AMERICA

AFRICA

THE UNITED STATES
Chinese and Japanese forms of Buddhism are strong in the U.S. In the 1960s a Chinese scholar, Hsuan Ha, established an international Buddhist community in Talmage, California, called The City of Ten Thousand Buddhas. Books about Zen made it more widely known. There are Zen centers in New York and Hawaii. A lama who fled from Tibet in 1959 and arrived in the U.S. in 1969 set up a Tibetan Buddhist institute in Boulder, Colorado.

GREAT BRITAIN
The Buddhist Society was founded in 1907, but became strong in 1924 under the leadership of Christmas Humphreys (1901–83). Humphreys was a lawyer and judge. He wrote several books about Buddhism and made radio and television broadcasts. Today the Society publishes a journal.

All types of Buddhism are represented in Great Britain—Theravada, Tibetan, Soto Zen, Rinzai Zen, Pure Land.

SOUTH AMERICA
There are followers of Buddhism in Argentina, Brazil, and Peru.

Key

■ countries where **Buddhism is the main religion**

□ countries where **there are significant numbers of followers of Buddhism**

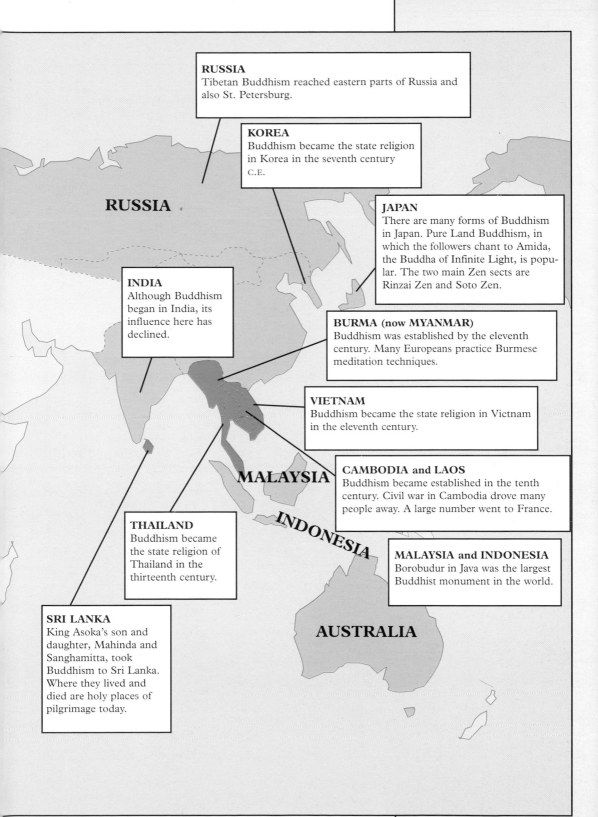

RUSSIA
Tibetan Buddhism reached eastern parts of Russia and also St. Petersburg.

KOREA
Buddhism became the state religion in Korea in the seventh century C.E.

JAPAN
There are many forms of Buddhism in Japan. Pure Land Buddhism, in which the followers chant to Amida, the Buddha of Infinite Light, is popular. The two main Zen sects are Rinzai Zen and Soto Zen.

INDIA
Although Buddhism began in India, its influence here has declined.

BURMA (now MYANMAR)
Buddhism was established by the eleventh century. Many Europeans practice Burmese meditation techniques.

VIETNAM
Buddhism became the state religion in Vietnam in the eleventh century.

CAMBODIA and LAOS
Buddhism became established in the tenth century. Civil war in Cambodia drove many people away. A large number went to France.

THAILAND
Buddhism became the state religion of Thailand in the thirteenth century.

MALAYSIA and INDONESIA
Borobudur in Java was the largest Buddhist monument in the world.

SRI LANKA
King Asoka's son and daughter, Mahinda and Sanghamitta, took Buddhism to Sri Lanka. Where they lived and died are holy places of pilgrimage today.

RUSSIA

MALAYSIA

INDONESIA

AUSTRALIA

A MONASTERY IN NORTHEAST THAILAND

Koon lives with his parents, brothers, and sisters in a wooden house on stilts. Nearby live his grandparents, aunts, uncles, and cousins. For his mother's birthday, they go to the forest monastery to offer rice, fruit, and vegetables for a meal.

It is already hot as they cross the fields, but within the shrine room it is cool. The huge brass Buddha, surrounded by flowers, is gleaming. In the kitchen the local people cook on charcoal stoves. When the food is ready, it is taken to the shrine room, where the monks sit cross-legged on a raised platform.

Everyone bows three times to the "Buddha, Dharma, *Sangha.*" Koon helps lift the food containers, one by one, to the abbot, who first helps himself and then passes the food to the next monk. When all the monks have taken what they need, the food is passed to the lay people. After a blessing, they take the food to the spacious kitchen, sit on mats in family groups, and share the food. What is left will be carried in bamboo baskets to the old and sick.

Koon's family returns to talk to the abbot, who wishes the mother long life and happiness. Koon feels fine going home, his stomach full of good food.

A monastery in Thailand with typical curved roofs

A MONASTERY IN ENGLAND

"On a Sunday visit to the monastery with my mum, I play on the field with the other children while she helps in the kitchen. A bell reminds us to get ready for the meal. At 10:30 A.M. we go to the *sala*, the big meeting room, to offer food to the monks and nuns. We serve it quietly and carefully as they walk along the line of people. After offering the food, we sit on the floor while the monks and nuns chant a blessing. Then we are invited to eat. Usually we give fruit and cakes, but Asian families bring interesting, varied food. I specially like yellow Thai potatoes. We really have a feast!

"Soon I am coming on a Family Weekend. Our parents organize drama and painting workshops and circle dancing. To my surprise, I like dancing. If it is fine at night we will sit around a campfire, drinking steaming cups of cocoa. The dharma classes are good, because the monks and nuns make Buddhism really interesting and show us how to meditate. I used to think they looked funny in their robes. Now I feel they are my special friends."

Learning how to meditate at a Theravada monastery in England

Tibetans turn prayer wheels to send blessings to the world.

Tibetan Buddhism

Tibetan Buddhism is colorful, with numerous gods and goddesses, brightly decorated temples, dances in elaborate costumes to frighten away evil spirits, music with unusual instruments, and many rituals. These are all part of the Tibetans' sincere trust in the Buddha. Their religion is woven into their daily lives.

Everywhere, prayer wheels containing special prayers are turned to send help to all living beings. Prayer flags flutter in the wind. There are holy chants called mantras. The most sacred is:

Om Mani Padme Hüm
(Hail to the Jewel in the Lotus).

In Tibetan Buddhism there are four, rather than three, Refuges: "Buddha, Dharma, *Sangha*, and the Guru." The guru is a personal teacher in whom the pupil must have complete trust.

Zen Buddhism

For Zen Buddhists, practicing archery is a way of meditating. People can bring meditation into many of their daily activities.

Zen Buddhism was taken from China to Japan, Korea, and Vietnam. Zen monks work and practice diligently. In the *zendo*, the meditation hall, each monk has a small space for sitting, eating, and sleeping. The monks can meditate as they take part in activities such as judo and other martial arts, flower arrangment called *ikebana*, tea ceremonies, and gardening.

A unique feature of Rinzai Zen Buddhism is the koan. Koans are problems about which the monks meditate; but they cannot be answered by the ordinary rational mind. They take the thinker beyond the limit of intellect. A famous example is: "What is the sound of one hand clapping?"

3

THE SCRIPTURES

For four hundred years after the Buddha's death the sermons, stories, and *Vinaya* (rules of conduct) were remembered and passed on orally by monks and nuns. Then they were written down in the Pali language, and they comprise the Theravada teaching, the Pali Canon. Many more stories were written in Sanskrit, and these formed part of the vast number of Mahayana teachings; further Mahayana teaching came from Tibet, China, and Japan. Today, all the teachings have been translated into most major languages.

There are many similarities between Pali and Sanskrit, both languages from India. Today, they are used in religion, but not in everyday speech.

Some important teachings

One important teaching is the Three Signs of Being:

- Life is always changing.

- I suffer when I expect life to be always the way I like it.

- I change also. What I call "myself" is not fixed, not a permanent self.

The eight spokes of the dharma wheel represent the Eightfold Path to Enlightenment. This is also called the Middle Way, between extreme asceticism and worldliness.

Another is about karma, which means "action." Whatever people do, good or bad, will bring results. When people are said to have bad karma, it means that they have the results of bad actions.

The dharma wheel

The Buddha's first sermon, in which he explained the Four Noble Truths, is called "The First Turning of the Dharma Wheel." The dharma wheel is a symbol for the way out of suffering, the Eightfold Path.

SUBLIME STATES

The Buddha said that people had within them four beautiful qualities:

- *Metta*—Loving kindness

- *Karuna*—Compassion

- *Mudita*—Joy in another's happiness

- *Upekkha*—Balance and peace whatever happens

These are known as the *Brahma Viharas*, the sublime states.

THE METTA SUTRA

This is part of the Buddha's words on *Metta*:

This is what should be done
By one who is skilled in goodness,
And who knows the path of peace:
Let him be able and upright,
Straightforward and gentle in speech.
Humble and not conceited,
Contented and easily satisfied.
Unburdened with duties and frugal in his ways.
Peaceful and calm, and wise and skillful,
Not proud and demanding in nature.
Let him not do the slightest thing
That the wise would later reprove.
Wishing: In gladness and in safety,
May all beings be at ease!
Whatever living beings there may be;
Whether they are weak or strong, omitting none,
The great or the mighty, medium, short or small,
The seen and the unseen,
Those living near and far away,
Those born and to-be-born—
May all beings be at ease.
Let none deceive another,
Or despise any being in any state.
Let none through anger or ill-will
Wish harm upon another.
Even as a mother protects with her life
Her child, her only child,
So with a boundless heart
Should one cherish all living beings;
Radiating kindness over the entire world:
Spreading upward to the skies,
And downward to the depths;
Outward and unbounded,
Freed from hatred and ill-will.

(From the *Sutra Nipata*)

The Tibetan Wheel of Life

This frightening wheel symbol is held by Yama, the Lord of Change. It is said to be a map of six states of the mind: Heaven, the Angry Gods, the Hungry Ghosts, Hell, the Animal State, and the Human State. From moment to moment in their minds, people can move through these states: joyful, angry and bossy, unsatisfied, wretched, thoughtless, and able to see clearly. The Human State, in which people are able to see clearly, is the best state to be in for reaching enlightenment.

In the middle, a pig, a rooster, and a snake keep the wheel turning. They represent ignorance, greed, and hatred. A famous sermon of the Buddha called them the Three Fires. They cause *dukkha* (suffering) in individuals and in the world. When the Three Fires die down completely, there is peace and freedom. That is the motionless point at the very center of the wheel.

A Tibetan Wheel of Life, painted on a temple wall in Ladakh, India.

THE ELEPHANT

The Buddha told this story when the *bhikkshus* reported to him that holy men were quarreling about their beliefs.

Once a king invited all the blind men to his palace. Then he asked his servant to bring an elephant. The servant did so and said, "An elephant is like this," and told each blind man to feel a different part of the animal. Then the king came and asked the blind men what an elephant was like.

Those who had felt the head said, "Sire, the elephant is like a jar." Those who had felt the ear said, "It is like a winnowing basket." The tusk was likened to a post, the trunk to a plow's pole, the body to a granary, the foot to the base of a column, the rump to a mortar, the tail to a pestle, and the tuft of the tail to a broom. Then they started to quarrel. "I'm right. You are wrong." And this led to fighting.

The Buddha said that those who insist that what they believe is right and everyone else is wrong are like the blind men who thought that a part of the elephant was the whole.

THE MAHAYANA TEACHING

Early Buddhism concentrated on practice in the monasteries. However, lay people wished to participate more and to feel that they, too, could be enlightened, and so the new Mahayana teaching developed.

In Mahayana Buddhism, bodhisattvas are compassionate beings who are ready to be enlightened and to enter nirvana, but who choose instead to help other people. The teaching says that all beings have the "Buddha nature" of compassion and wisdom within themselves. They can find nirvana in the changing world, samsara.

In Tibetan Buddhism, the Dalai Lama is considered to be the reincarnation of the bodhisattva Avalokiteshvara.

How the scriptures are used

People were practicing Buddhism before it was common to be able to read. Stories from the scriptures were painted on the temple walls, and people listened carefully to the *sangha*'s teaching. Many memorized and chanted the important sermons with the monks—and many people still do this.

Today, the central scriptures are taught in every type of Buddhism. In monasteries the monks and nuns continue the tradition of giving talks without written notes. When requested to teach, they sit quietly until the right words enter their mind. They "let the dharma speak." They also answer questions as the Buddha did.

The bodhisattva Avalokiteshvara. This sixteenth-century Tibetan figure shows the bodhisattva on a lotus throne and making the anjali *gesture. The bodhisattva ideal gives people a god or goddess of compassion to emulate. They try to do this by practicing the six perfections: generosity, morality, patience, vigor, meditation, wisdom.*

4

HOME AND FAMILY LIFE

Dana

Generosity is very important in Buddhism. *Dana* means "generosity" or "gift." When the first monks and nuns were ordained two thousand five hundred years ago, they renounced money and relied on generous people to supply their needs. Today this continues. Theravada lay Buddhists give food to monks on *pindapata* (the alms round), or they take a gift of food to the monastery to add to that collected in the morning.

There are other ways to help, too: cooking, washing dishes, cleaning the brass, putting fresh flowers on the shrine, gardening, and so on. It is usual for lay Buddhists to provide the *sangha* with food and with essential goods: clothes, medicine, and everyday things such as toothpaste, toilet paper, and detergent.

Many people participated in giving dana *to the* sangha *at this celebration at a Theravada monastery. Each gave a token gift of rice.*

By providing the monks and nuns with what they need to live, people give them the opportunity to live harmlessly, meditating and seeking the truth. In return, the *sangha* gives people the benefit of the dharma (teaching) and of a spiritual example. *Dana* therefore forges a very close link between the monastery community and lay Buddhists.

A family gives food to monks.

PINDAPATA *IN THE CITY*

At 5:30 A.M., Bangkok, the capital of Thailand, is already busy with traffic and people. After morning *puja* (worship), hundreds of *bhikkshus* walk silently on *pindapata*. All over this large city, many people await the *bhikkshus* with rice, fruit, and small packets of food wrapped in banana leaves. Everyone puts an offering in the bowls, then bows, hands together in *anjali*. The *bhikkshus* return to their temples and the people hurry to their homes or to stores, offices, and factories to do their day's work. They have started the day with a generous action.

PINDAPATA *IN A VILLAGE*

Early every morning in Thailand, many villagers wait patiently at the roadside for the *bhikkshus* to walk by on *pindapata*. When the *bhikkshus* arrive—barefoot, holding their alms bowls, eyes lowered—the people kneel and place an offering of food into each bowl. The *bhikkshus* do not express thanks, because Buddhists believe that giving is more perfect without thanks. Each person bows as a gesture of respect. The saffron-robed figures move away along the dusty road and people return to their homes, happy to have contributed to the *bhikkshus*' only meal of the day.

Contact with the monastery

Families go to the monastery, and monks and nuns come into family homes for special occasions, such as the blessing of a new baby, a newly married couple, or a new house; or to visit someone who is sick or dying. There is a *dana* meal, followed by a special chanting to bring the good powers of the universe into the family.

People are always welcome at a monastery. They can join the community for morning and evening *puja* (worship), or they can meditate alone. Some monasteries with a lot of extra rooms invite families to stay. In France, a Vietnamese Zen monk has a center called Plum Village where families and single people can live together for a time in the Buddhist way of mindfulness.

Most people go to work and most children go to school, so Sunday is a good day to visit a monastery as a family and to share a *dana* meal. People meet friends and talk to *sangha* members. Family days are popular, when children learn about Buddhism through stories, acting, and drawing. They can practice meditation with a monk or nun. Some monasteries and centers have regular Sunday school for children and workshops for adults. It is not easy to sit for a long time, and so children practice sitting and walking meditation and discuss any problems they have.

On festival days families go to the monastery with food to share in a *dana* feast. They put up decorations, flags, and lanterns. The holy days in a monastery are the full moon days. Some people spend the whole day at the monastery, dressed in white for the occasion. They ask for the Refuges and Precepts and may even meditate all night with the monks and nuns.

Puja *and meditation at home*

Puja and meditation can take place at home. A family will set up a shrine in part of a room or in a separate little room. On the shrine will be a *buddharupa*, candles, incense, and fresh flowers. These remind

BLESSING A HOME

To bless a new home, a *bhikkshu* uses a bowl of water, a *buddharupa* (a statue of the Buddha), a candle and matches, and some flowers.

In front of the family, he lights the candle and drips candle wax into the water while chanting blessings. This brings together the four basic elements: earth, air, fire, and water.

The *bhikkshu* then flicks the holy water over everyone with the flowers and goes into every room, chanting and flicking water in the same way. Those present feel that the house has been truly blessed and that it will be a happy Buddhist home.

The Buddha made no strict rules, but gave these precepts for daily life:

- To try not to harm living beings.

- To try not to steal.

- To try not to use sexuality to harm oneself or others.

- To try not to tell lies or call people names.

- To try not to use drink or drugs that harm mind and body.

them of the Buddha and of the goodness everyone can develop. The flowers will naturally fade and change, just as all things change. Some Buddhists also put water and small offerings of food on the shrine. It is usual to bow to the shrine in respect and gratitude to the Buddha and as a sign of humility. The family sits in front of the shrine, chanting and meditating together.

If they have time, families will try to meditate in the morning and the evening, sitting in silence together, hands in laps, eyes partly or entirely closed. But the Buddha said that people can meditate when they stand, walk, or lie down. They can also be mindful throughout the day, during work, play, waiting for a bus, walking to school, eating, and lying down to sleep.

Young children are not compelled to meditate. Older children are encouraged to imagine that, whenever they sit in meditation, they are sitting beneath the Bodhi tree, as the Buddha did.

Applying Buddhism to daily life

Parents try to help their children understand the importance of always showing respect and generosity to all people.

Right Work is an important part of the Eightfold Path, and the first of the Five Moral Precepts is to try not to harm living beings. It would be wrong livelihood for a Buddhist to slaughter animals or to make or sell war weapons. Work connected with gambling or charging high interest on loans would also be wrong livelihood. Work should do no harm and, ideally, should help people. Teaching, building homes, and helping in conserving the natural world are some examples.

Because of the first Moral Precept, monks and nuns and many lay people would, by choice, be vegetarian. However, monks and nuns must accept whatever food they are given, even if it is meat.

5

MONASTERIES

The Buddha attracted followers who shared his austere life. They were *dhutanga* monks, wandering holy men who depended on alms food for survival. For shelter in the rainy season, they built a dwelling place called a *vihara*, or monastery.

Gradually more *viharas* were built, and then larger and larger ones. Monks took the dharma to other countries, where different rules and rituals were developed. Now Buddhism is a world religion with vast differences, like a tree with many branches. Monks still live in remote forests or high in the mountains, but many others live in city monasteries as scholars and teachers.

Whatever the differences, most monks and nuns shave their heads, wear simple robes, and have few possessions. These are signs that they have renounced vanity.

Lay Buddhists have five Moral Precepts to follow. For the *sangha*, there are 227 Precepts, designed to help them live together without harming the environment. These are listed and explained in the *Vinaya* (rules of conduct). Early nuns had 84 more precepts just for women.

Three traditions, one religion: Jisu Sunim (left) from Korea is Zen; Geshe Tashi (center) is a Tibetan gelug; and Ajahn Sumedho from the United States is a senior bhikkshu *in the Theravada tradition.*

Monks and nuns renounce possessions and keep only what is necessary. When Buddhism began, the eight necessary items were a robe, an alms bowl, a belt, a razor, a needle, a filter for straining drinking water, a staff, and a toothpick.

When monks and nuns are ordained today, they receive some of these items, but they also receive other essentials such as umbrellas or warm coats.

Daily life in the monastery

In any monastery, daily life is rigorous, with much work to do. No one is too proud to do menial tasks. The aim is to learn to do everything mindfully and skillfully.

Novice monks at work stacking bricks in a forest monastery, Ko Samui, Thailand.

A DAY IN A THERAVADA MONASTERY

In a Theravada monastery in northeast Thailand, the bell rings at 3:00 A.M. Morning *puja* and meditation are followed by *pindapata*. Every day the monastery is cleaned and the paths are swept. After a blessing, the monks eat their daily meal in silence. In a remote monastery there may be no piped water or electricity. Water is drawn from a well. Monks sew their own robes and boil dye for them. When not working, they meditate in "kutis," small wooden huts in the forest. The day ends with evening *puja* and meditation.

Why do men and women choose this demanding life? They consider enlightenment to be the most important aim for a human being. They may wish to dedicate their lives to the development of absolute purity, or they may want to help people by teaching the dharma and supporting them through life's problems.

A novice nun and a well-cared-for cat at a Bangkok monastery

Tibetan monks clearing snow in China

STUDY IN A TIBETAN MONASTERY

In a Tibetan monastery, monks get up at 5:00 A.M. and meditate for two hours. After breakfast and prayers, they study and learn sacred texts by heart. One feature of Tibetan training is energetic debating, which tests monks' knowledge. They debate after the midday meal. There are further sessions of study and debate before the evening meal, then study and meditation before bed. Boys can enter the monastery between the ages of seven and twelve, and those seeking high achievement study for fifteen years. After exams, some study for five more years. Now that the Tibetans are in exile, large numbers of monks cannot be supported, because the people are too poor.

Tibetan monks debate difficult and profound points of the teaching vehemently but without anger.

A SOTO ZEN MONASTERY

The young men in a Soto Zen monastery, high in the mountains of Japan, have already studied Buddhism in college. They wake up at 4:30 A.M. for meditation at 4:45. Each monk has a small space on a platform where he meditates, eats, and sleeps. He meditates sitting on a round black cushion and facing a wall. After meditation he chants "The Heart Sutra," a famous sermon. Breakfast is followed by a day of hard work, scrubbing and polishing to make the monastery spick-and-span, and laboring on the land. There are long sessions of meditation.

In the Soto Zen tradition, meditators sit facing a wall.

Novices, monks, and abbots

Novices in a Theravada monastery can be ordained after two years. They wear white. For the ordination, the whole *sangha* assembles in a special area called a *sima*. Sponsors, usually relatives, present the novices with new saffron robes and alms bowls. They request admittance to the *sangha* from the abbot, who is the head of the monastery, and then retire to put on their new robes. After a long ceremony in Pali, they are admitted to the *sangha* and are given new names. Friends bring them gifts and wish them well.

TITLES FOR MONKS

After ten years, a *bhikkshu* is called *Ajahn* (teacher). *Ajahns* are often in charge of monasteries. Another high title is *Chao Khun*, which means "abbot."

Each tradition has its own titles. In Tibetan Buddhism an ordinary monk is a *gelong*, one who studies and passes exams is a *geshe*, and a senior member is a lama. A *tulku* is a boy lama (see page 11).

In Zen, a *roshi* is a teacher in the monastery. The *jūshoku* is the head monk. The abbot is called *kanchō*. Very famous masters who have passed on the teaching are called patriarchs. It is said that there have been 28 patriarchs, of which the Buddha was the first.

Becoming ordained

In the West people are ordained when they are adults, but in Far Eastern countries boys have their heads shaved and wear robes. They are educated by the monks, and some of them decide to be monks for the rest of their lives. Many return to lay life.

In the Theravada tradition, many young men become monks, if only for a few weeks or months. It is thought to be a good training for life. The present king of Thailand was a monk for a short time.

On the other hand, elderly people, who feel that their duties as lay people are completed may be ordained and end their days in a monastery.

Not all Buddhist monks and nuns take vows to remain in the robe for life, though many do. They are free to leave and return to lay life.

Originally, all Buddhist monks had to remain unmarried. Today, if they want to marry, Theravada monks and nuns must still leave the *sangha*, but some Zen and Tibetan monks are married and remain as monks.

Novice Buddhist monks in Sri Lanka

Nuns

The Buddha ordained *bhikkshunis*, and the tradition lasted for hundreds of years. There were many outstanding Buddhist nuns. Then the tradition ended and was never revived. Perhaps the nuns perished in war or famine. Afterward, women became Theravada novices but were never ordained, remaining in a lowly position. In the Mahayana tradition women were ordained, but not many had high positions.

However, times changed. In Western countries, women who follow the Theravada tradition have received a form of ordination, though not as *bhikkshunis*. They wear brown robes, live by strict rules, and, like *bhikkshus*, have few possessions. They go on *pindapata*, teach lay people, and are highly respected.

Many women are now meditation teachers, and more and more wish to be ordained and to be fully trained.

At the end of their ordination ceremony, two Theravada nuns stand holding their new alms bowls.

Women of the Soto Zen tradition in the West are absolutely equal with men. In fact, both men and women are called monks. The founder of monasteries and many Buddhist centers practicing Soto Zen is a woman, Reverend Master Jiyu Kennett. Her main monastery is in the United States. Venerable Myokyo-ni, another woman, founded a Rinzai Zen center in London.

Jeanne Bendik is from California, and has been a "student of the Buddha's teachings" (she prefers this to calling herself a Buddhist) for fifteen years. She lived on retreat for a year at the Insight Meditation Society center in Barre, Massachusetts, and then stayed for a further eighteen months as a volunteer worker. She says:

"I see the Buddha's teaching as a road map for understanding how we create our own unhappiness and therefore can end a good bit of that unhappiness. I continue to learn about how my actions and choices cause pain and suffering, or 'unsatisfactoriness.' The practice of meditation is the most valuable tool for learning about our minds and for changing behavior patterns that are unskillful.

"At monasteries in the United States, the monks and nuns are usually Thai or Sri Lankan. There are few monasteries where Western monks and nuns give the teachings. More people in the United States learn about Buddhism at meditation retreat centers, where lay people, many of whom have spent time as monks, are very good at communicating the Eastern teachings in a way that is accessible to the Western mind."

Receiving a blessing at a monastery

Lay Buddhists of all traditions go on retreats. They stay at a monastery or meditation center for a week or longer to meditate and live together mindfully and quietly. In a monastery, a blessing is usually given at the end of a retreat. The monk or nun in charge brings together the four elements, as described in blessing the home on page 25. A thin string is then stretched from the *buddharupa* to the bowl of water, then to the *sangha* members and lay people. During chanting of the paritta (blessings), they gently hold the string. The string is then wound, people are sprinkled with the water, and the string is cut into short pieces and tied around the wrist of each lay person. This is a reminder of the retreat and the blessing and is worn until the string wears away and drops off.

Monks on tudong

The Buddha and his disciples were *dhutanga* monks, homeless wanderers receiving alms food and teaching the dharma. *Tudong* means doing the same. When monks and nuns go on *tudong* today, they set out on a long walk that lasts two weeks or longer, in twos or threes or alone. They then are truly homeless, dependent on the good will of the people they meet. They obey rules of the countryside and never stay anywhere without permission. Farmers usually let them sleep in barns or sheds, or put up a tent. Buddhists invite them to their homes. Some lay people meet them with food for a picnic and, after the meal, walk part of the way with them. This is a good way for monks and lay people to meet and to encourage mutual understanding.

Leaving on tudong. *Backpacking monks of today follow an old tradition.*

LIFE CYCLE

Buddhists like to share events in their lives with the monks and nuns and with one another.

Birth

In the West, the date of birth and the name of each baby are officially registered, but many parents want a religious ceremony as well. Buddhist parents take their baby to a monastery. They can request a religious name with a beautiful meaning for their child. Then the monks and nuns chant many blessings: for protection, health, happiness, and noble qualities.

A monk flicks holy water over a new baby and its family at the blessing.

Marriage

In a Soto Zen monastery in the West, a couple may have a Buddhist marriage ceremony. A couple from the United States were shown on television being given a Tibetan marriage ceremony in India. However, such ceremonies are rather unusual.

AN UNUSUAL COMING-OF-AGE

In Buddhism there is no special ritual for boys and girls when they reach adulthood. But this is what happened when a young boy requested that his coming-of-age be marked. Edward had been going to the *vihara* (monastery) for 12 years and the abbot felt that his intentions were good and that his life would benefit from having such a ceremony.

"On March 12 I celebrated my thirteenth birthday at the *vihara*. I decided to do this because my cousin and my friend are having a Bar Mitzvah (a Jewish religious coming of age) this year. I decided that I would like to celebrate my thirteenth birthday in a Buddhist way. I invited lots of people. It was a celebration of the beginning of my adult years. The day before, I stayed at the *vihara* and helped

with various jobs. I also prepared myself for the day ahead. The day started with the offering of a *dana* meal to the monks, followed by *paritta* chanting, precepts, and a short dharma talk by Ajahn Santacitto. All of these I requested in Pali. We had blessings and people offered reflections on what it means to be a man. After the ceremony we planted a Douglas fir tree to remind us of the occasion. We had found this tree growing in our front garden. Lots of people gave me presents, including a *buddharupa* from the monks at the *vihara*."

(Edward Walters, age 13)

Edward's coming-of-age.

More usually, in Theravada Buddhism, a couple will go to a monastery after a legal marriage ceremony and offer a *dana* meal to the *sangha* and their friends. They are given the Refuges and Precepts, and a special blessing is chanted for their future life together.

Death

All Buddhists believe that life consists of beginnings and endings, constant change. People are always experiencing the birth and death of ideas, moods, and conditions in themselves. Knowing this, people accept the death of the body as a natural result of being born. It is part of the rhythm of the whole universe. Buddhists believe that it is possible to be enlightened even in the last moment of life.

When they know that they are dying, some people request to go to a monastery to die. For those at home or in a hospital, the monks and nuns visit them to chant the blessings for the dying.

Children join the family, friends, and bhikkshus *around a funeral pyre in Thailand.*

After a death, a ceremony is held in which a relative or friend of the dead person pours water into an empty bowl, which overflows into a dish below. These words are recited:

Let the pure thoughts of goodwill
    be shared by my relative
    and may he/she be happy.
As water runs from the rivers to
    fill the ocean,
So may well-being and merit within us
Pour forth and reach our beloved
    departed one.

In many traditional Buddhist countries, dead bodies are burned rather than buried. A body is not taken to a crematorium but to a monastery, where it is burned on a funeral pyre.

The Shanti stupa, Ladakh, India (above) and the Shwedagon stupa, Rangoon, Myanmar

Stupas

In all Buddhist countries there are burial mounds that contain relics of the Buddha and of great masters. At first they were made of earth covered with brick. Through the years they became larger, beautifully carved, and adorned with gold. When a great master died recently in Thailand, a splendid monument was erected. These monuments are called stupas in Theravada countries, pagodas in China and Japan, and *chörten* in Tibet. They are now being built in some monasteries in Europe.

FESTIVALS

= Theravada

= Tibetan

= Zen

Buddhist countries use a different calendar from the West. The months on this chart of major festivals are approximate equivalents. Some festivals existed before Buddhism, and Buddhist meaning has been added to them. One such event is New Year. It is not celebrated at the same time in every country.

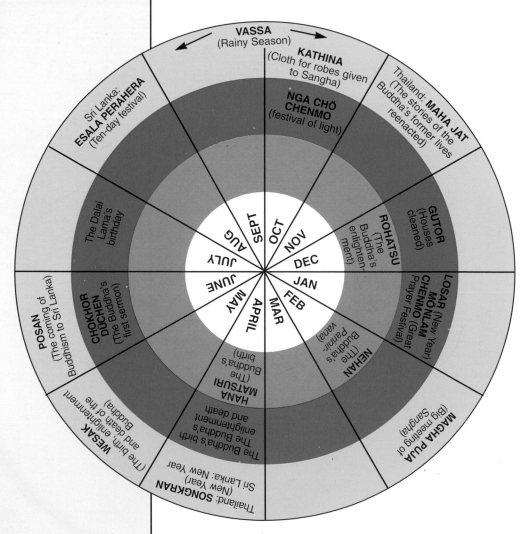

Tibetan festivals

In preparation for New Year, people thoroughly clean their houses and perform rituals to drive out evil spirits. Then the year begins with three days of feasting, dancing, and sports, followed by three weeks of more serious ceremonies during the Great Prayer Festival. Before the Chinese invasion of Tibet, thousands of monks gathered in Lhasa for these traditions.

To celebrate the Buddha's birth, enlightenment, and death, ceremonies are held in the monasteries. Some people fast, but there is also fun: picnics, dancing, acting, and sports.

An especially happy celebration is the birthday of the Dalai Lama. At Nga Chö Chenmo, thousands of lamps are lit in honor of a great Tibetan scholar.

FULL MOON

In different Buddhist countries, each full moon can bring a separate celebration. In Theravada monasteries, monks and nuns meditate all night at each full moon. At the other phases of the moon they sit in meditation until midnight. Lay Buddhists may join them.

Tibetan Buddhists in Gansu, China, go to the temple for New Year prayers.

Zen festivals

The three main Zen Buddhist festivals celebrate the birth, the enlightenment, and the death of the Buddha. The *Hana Matsuri* festival for the birth of the Buddha is joyful. Images of a child Buddha are placed on beautifully decorated shrines. A legend in Japan tells how six dragons sprinkled the baby Buddha with perfume. The Japanese make a special perfumed tea and wash the Buddha images with it. This tea is reputed to heal the sick, so people try to obtain some for their sick relatives. At the rituals for this festival, the Zen monks wear splendid robes.

Remembering the Buddha's enlightenment at the *Rohatsu* festival, monks try to sit for a whole day and night in intensive meditation.

In the *Nehran* festival, the remembrance of the Buddha's *Parinirvana* (final death), temple lights are extinguished, and monks meditate and chant in the dark. The lights are relit as a symbol that the light of the Buddha's truth and wisdom will continue to shine.

Children in Japan take part in the joyful festival celebrating the Buddha's birth.

Theravada festivals

Thais and Sri Lankans celebrate New Year with religious ceremonies and also processions, music, and dancing.

Magha Puja commemorates the spontaneous coming together of 1,250 disciples of the Buddha. The Buddha gave them a special teaching, of which this is a part:

> The not doing of all evils,
> The doing of what is wholly good,
> The cleansing of one's own heart,
> These are the teachings of all the Buddhas.

Esala Perahera is a ten-day festival during which a relic of the Buddha in a golden casket is carried on a huge elephant. A lighted procession with dancers, acrobats, splendid costumes, and one hundred elephants is a breathtaking spectacle.

Monks therefore meet at the main monastery for discussion, meditation, and dharma teaching. Lay people may join them.

At the end of *vassa* (the rainy season), *Kathina*, a big alms-giving ceremony, is celebrated. Cloth for robes is given to the monks. A worthy monk is chosen to receive a new robe, and other monks go away to make it before the day ends. Many gifts are given and people fasten money to a "money tree."

The main Theravada festival, however, is *Wesak*. *Wesak* celebrates the birth, enlightenment, and death of the Buddha, all in one day.

Wesak *in the West*

Wesak in Western countries follows many of the traditions of the East, such as decorating the monastery with Buddhist flags, lanterns, and flowers, and wearing white. People chant the Refuges and Precepts, listen to chanting, share a *dana* meal, and listen to a talk. A cheerful day of generosity and friendliness is followed by an evening of meditation. At night, people walk around the stupa three times, remembering "Buddha, Dharma, *Sangha*," and leave offerings of candles, incense, and flowers. Some lay Buddhists meditate all night with the *sangha*.

Wesak *in Sri Lanka*

On the morning of *Wesak*, people all over Sri Lanka dress in white and carry baskets of flowers to the monastery. Those who intend to practice all day take ten precepts instead of the usual five. The five extra precepts are not to eat after noon, not to sing, not to dance, not to wear jewelry, and not to sleep on a luxurious bed.

Collecting lotus flowers for Wesak *in Sri Lanka. The lotus flower is a symbol of purity in Buddhism. The Buddha is often depicted seated on a lotus.*

Everyone gives alms to the *sangha* and to the poor. In many places free food and drinks are offered. Some people give blood donations to hospitals. Very generous people have had dharma books printed for free distribution. *Wesak* cards are sent to relatives and friends.

CELEBRATING THE BUDDHA'S BIRTHDAY IN KOREA

Today is the eighth day of the fourth month, according to the lunar calendar. It is Buddha's birthday, so the Kim family will go to their favorite monastery. It is far away, deep in the mountains, so they will stay overnight. As they arrive, they pay their respects to the monk in charge of the guest rooms by putting their hands together and doing a half bow. Then they all go to the main Buddha hall and bow deep down to the ground three times to the Buddha. They have their names written on a piece of paper, which will be stuck on a paper lantern, and they give a donation as a way of obtaining merit and giving blessing to the whole family. After the meal, they go to evening prayers in the main Buddha hall, and then they help light the paper lanterns. What a beautiful sight it is in the depth of the night: all these lanterns attached on ropes across the courtyard.

(Account by Martine Batchelor, who was a nun in Korea)

It is also a great arts festival. Children ride on decorated floats, singing Buddhist songs and carrying lanterns. There are special TV and radio programs. Poets, actors, singers, and dancers are encouraged to perform. Artists paint pictures. All the songs, poems, plays, and pictures center on the Buddha, his former lives, and events in Sri Lankan history.

Everything reflects the goodness and compassion of the Buddhas—for it is said that there have been many Buddhas in the past. When people forget the teaching, another Buddha will come to show the way of the Eightfold Path.

Wesak at Anuradhapura, Sri Lanka. Buddhists light candles and oil lamps, which symbolize the Buddha's enlightenment.

Glossary

The Buddha's teachings were first written in two Indian languages, Pali and Sanskrit. Mahayana Buddhists use Sanskrit (S) and Theravada Buddhists use Pali (P). Sanskrit terms are more commonly used in America.

alms — gift of food or money to the poor.

anjali — gesture of respect and greeting, hands together.

bhikkshu (S), *bhikkhu* (P) — Buddhist monk.

bhikkshuni (S), *bhikkhuni* (P) — Buddhist nun.

bodhi (S) — enlightenment.

Bodhi tree — Bo tree. The tree under which the Buddha sat when he was enlightened.

bodhisattva (S), **bodhisatta** (P) — god or goddess of compassion. Mahayana Buddhists take the Bodhisattva Vow to help all suffering beings.

Brahma Viharas — the four sublime states of mind: loving kindness, compassion, joy in others' happiness, balance and peace of mind.

Buddha — the awakened one, the one who knows.

Buddha, Dharma, Sangha — the Three Refuges.

buddharupa — statue of the Buddha.

chörten — (Tibetan) burial mound.

Dalai Lama — King of Tibet and spiritual leader of Tibetan Buddhists.

dana — generosity; a generous gift.

dharma (S), **dhamma** (P) — the Buddha's teaching, the natural law.

dhutanga — literally, a "means of shaking off." Living simply, which includes traveling without food or shelter and relying on what is given.

duhkha (S), *dukkha* (P) — suffering, unsatisfactoriness.

Hinayana — literally, "small vehicle." Name given to the older, traditional forms of Buddhism when Mahayana developed in the first century C.E.

karma (S), **kamma** (P) — action that leads to inevitable results. Good actions bring good results, and bad actions bring bad results.

karuna — compassion, one of the Brahma Viharas.

lama — "teacher": Tibetan monk.

lay Buddhist — a Buddhist who is not a monk or a nun.

Mahayana — literally, "great vehicle." Umbrella term for the new forms of Buddhism that developed from the first century C.E.

Mara — the devil, who tried to tempt the Buddha as he sat beneath the Bodhi tree.

metta — loving kindness, one of the Brahma Viharas.

mudita — joy in another's fortune, one of the Brahma Viharas.

nirvana (S), **nibbana** (P) — the state of enlightenment.

pagoda — burial mound, in Nepal, China, and Japan.

parinirvana (S), *parinibbana* (P) — the Buddha's final death.

paritta — chanting of blessings.

pindapata — the alms round; the monks and nuns walk around the community each morning and people give them food.

precept — not a strict rule, but a way of behaving that a Buddhist tries to follow.

puja	an act of worship.
samsara	the changing world; the cycle of birth, sickness, old age, and death.
sangha	the community of monks and nuns.
Siddhartha (S), **Sidhatta** (P)	the Indian prince who became the Buddha.
stupa	burial mound.
sutra (S), *sutta* (P)	text; the word of the Buddha.
trishna (S), *tanha* (P)	thirst, wanting, desire.
Theravada	literally, "the teaching of the Elders"; the only remaining form of early, traditional Buddhism.
tudong	to go on *tudong* (a Thai word) is to set out on a long walk, living simply, dependent on people's generosity for food and shelter. (See also *dhutanga*.)
tulku	reincarnated lama.
upeksa (S), *upekkha* (P)	balance of mind, one of the Brahma Viharas.
vassa	the rainy season, when monks and nuns stay in one place to meditate and study.
Wesak (or *Vesak*)	the full moon of April or May, which gives its name to the celebration of the birth, enlightenment, and death of the Buddha.
vihara	dwelling place; monastery.
Vinaya	rules for the community of bhikkshus.
Yama	the lord of change—also Mara.
Zen	meditation. The name is given to a form of Japanese Buddhism that concentrates on meditation.

Book List

Burland, C. A. *The Way of the Buddha.* Chester Springs, PA: Dufour Editions, 1988.

Coatsworth, Elizabeth. *The Cat Who Went to Heaven,* revised edition. New York: Aladdin Books, 1990. (A favorite Chinese story retold.)

Geography Department Staff. *Sri Lanka in Pictures.* Visual Geography. Minneapolis: Lerner Publications, 1988.

Hull, Robert. *Indian Stories.* Tales from Around the World. New York: Thomson Learning, 1994.

Kendra, Judith. *Tibetans.* Threatened Cultures. New York: Thomson Learning, 1994.

Kipling, Rudyard. *Kim.* Originally published 1901. New York: Puffin Books, 1987. (In the course of this novel, Kim, an orphaned street boy in India, helps a Tibetan lama.)

Landaw, Jonathan and Brooke, Janet. *Prince Siddhartha.* Boston: Wisdom Publications, 1984. (The life and work of the Buddha, with fantasy, magic, and mystery—not strictly factual.)

Morgan, Peggy. *Being a Buddhist.* North Pomfret, VT: Trafalgar Square, 1989.

Morris, Scott, ed. *Religions of the World.* Using and Understanding Maps. New York: Chelsea House, 1993.

Snelling, John. *Buddhist Festivals.* Holidays and Festivals. Vero Beach, FL: Rourke Corp., 1987.

Wangu, Madhu Bazaz. *Buddhism.* World Religions. New York: Facts on File, 1992.

Note on Dates

Each religion has its own system for counting the years of its history. The starting point may be related to the birth or death of a special person or an important event. In everyday life, today, when different communities have dealings with one another, they need to use the same counting system for setting dates in the future and writing accounts of the past. The Western system is now used throughout the world. It is based on Christian beliefs about Jesus: B.C. (Before Christ) and A.D. (*Anno Domini* = in the year of our Lord). Some members of the various world faiths use the common Western system, but, instead of A.D. and B.C., they say and write C.E. (in the Common Era) and B.C.E.(before the Common Era).

Index

DATE DUE